KU-105-568

BEDE SIXTH FORM
B000487

MEDIA POWER

Causes and Campaigns

Jenny Vaughan

W
FRANKLIN WATTS
LONDON•SYDNEY

First published in 2009 by
Franklin Watts
338 Euston Road
London NW1 3BH

Franklin Watts Australia
Level 17/207 Kent Street
Sydney NSW 2000

Copyright © Franklin Watts 2009

All rights reserved. No part of this publication may be reproduced,
stored in a retrieval system, or transmitted in any form or by any means,
electronic, mechanical, photocopying, recording or otherwise, without the
prior writtenpermission of the copyright holder.

Series editor: Julia Bird
Design: Nimbus Design

A CIP catalogue record for this book is available from the British Library.

ISBN 978 0 7496 8866 0

Dewey classification: 302.2'3

Picture credits:
Action Press/Rex Features: 13; Advertising Archives: 11, 26, 33; J. Scott Applewhite/AP/PA Photos: 40; Adrian
Arbib/Corbis: 21; Bettmann/Corbis: 18; Hubert Boesl/DPA/PA Photos: 15; Manuel Citak/Greenpeace: 31; Em-
manuel Dunnard/epa/Corbis: 17; Durand-Hudson-Langevin-Orbon/Sygma/Corbis: 39; Tod A Gipstein/Corbis: 34;
Louise Gubb/SABA/Corbis: 27. Fiona Hanson/PA Photos: 30; Jeremy Horner/Corbis: 19; Steven Ka-
zlowski/Ecoscene: 38. Owaki Kulia/Corbis: 22; Christopher Morris/Corbis: 36; Claudio Onorati/epa/Corbis: 41.
Thierry Orban/Corbis: 23; Warwick Page/Corbis: 12; Photos 12/Alamy: 25; Brian Branch Price/AP.PA Photos: 28;
Pulse PL/PA Photos: 29; Chris Radburn/PA Archive/PA Photos: 8. Reuters/Corbis: 20, 35; Rex Features: 24; Julian
Simmonds/Rex Features; 32; SIpa Press/Rex Features: 9, 14; Steve Starr/Corbis: 10; David Turnley/Corbis; 37;
Aubrey Wade/Panos: 16.

Every attempt has been made to clear copyright.
Should there be any inadvertent omission,
please apply to the publisher for rectification.

With thanks to Barry White at the Campaign for Press
and Broadcasting Freedom for help and advice (http://www.cpbf.org.uk)

Printed in Malaysia

Franklin Watts is a division of Hachette Children's Books,
an Hachette UK company.
www.hachette.co.uk

Contents

Campaigning and the media

Campaigns are activities that support or draw attention to a particular cause. All campaigns need people behind them, whether they donate money directly to the cause, or help to do the work of the campaign themselves. The best way to get supporters is to use the media to communicate with the world about the cause behind the campaign.

Which media?

The media includes magazines, newspapers, television and radio (known as broadcasting), the Internet and email, books, plays and films. Campaigns that involve national or international issues, such as combating world poverty, need to use media that will reach as many people as possible. These campaigns try to get national newspapers, radio and television stations interested in them by writing to them, ringing them up or sending them press releases.

Campaigns around much smaller, local issues – such as keeping a school or library open, or making a section of road safer – use locally based newspapers and local radio and television stations.

A local campaign, like this one against a new road bypass, needs the support of local papers and radio to attract people's attention.

Blogging on

Campaigners can also use the Internet to let people know about their cause. Many send out regular emails to supporters, or produce blogs and on-line news. Some groups even make their own films for television, which they can also post on their websites.

The media at work

A good journalist will do his or her best to find out as much about a campaign as possible – and may end up showing that campaigners are wrong about an issue, or are conducting a campaign badly. Both positive and negative media coverage play a vital role in letting people know what a campaign or cause is all about.

Media coverage of humanitarian crises, such as the civil war in the Darfur region of Sudan, encourages the public to give money to help refugees and puts political pressure on governments and aid agencies.

• *Up for discussion* •

How can campaigners choose the right media to give publicity to their cause?

Is it possible to run a campaign without involving the media? How?

Money talks

Public Relations (PR) is the business of getting a point of view across to the public, usually through the media. Wealthy campaigners can spend huge sums on PR. The result can sometimes be a one-sided, or even misleading, account of the facts.

The high cost of campaigning media

There are specialist PR companies that campaign in various ways, such as conducting surveys, organising conferences, publishing research and employing experts – all to get the 'right' information to the media. Good PR can help campaigners to lobby (try to influence) governments. It helps if they can show that they have public support.

Campaign giants

For example, until recently, the oil giant Exxon funded groups that campaigned to question the science of climate change – the view among scientists that burning fossil fuels such as oil and coal causes global warming. Exxon has since withdrawn this funding.

It is not just the business world that uses PR. In the United States, the three million supporters of the National Rifle Association (NRA) fund a US $100-million-a-year PR campaign against controlling gun ownership. Yet in the United States, the murder rate using guns is many times higher than in countries where guns are controlled.

The NRA has spent millions of member's dollars over the years to convince people that there is no connection between wide ownership of guns and high levels of deaths by shooting. However, many people, like these protestors, remain unconvinced.

Case study: Tobacco

In the 1950s, health experts began warning that smoking causes diseases – in particular lung cancer. The tobacco industry hired expensive PR firms to challenge this and, with their help, set up the Council for Tobacco Research, headed by a scientist. But, in 1993, it was claimed in court that the work of the Council was actually 'part of an industry-wide strategy to mislead and confuse the public'. By the 1960s, the tobacco industry was paying as much as $20 million a year to argue its case. Later, it spent millions campaigning to make people doubt the dangers of breathing in other people's smoke (passive smoking). In spite of this, smoking in public places has now been banned in many countries.

Over the years, tobacco companies spent millions of dollars on promoting smoking as a normal, healthy activity.

• Up for discussion •

Can you think of any media campaigns that use PR, such as surveys and research, to convince you of something? Do they work, in your opinion?

Disaster!

When charities campaign for money after a disaster, they find the amount of media coverage the disaster receives makes a big difference. The support they get from the media depends partly on how serious the disaster is – but also on where it happens and who is affected.

Case study: Familiar places

In December 2004, a massive tsunami struck the Indian Ocean coast, killing around 300,000 people, including many European and American tourists. Media campaigns in the countries that the tourists came from gave this event huge coverage, bombarding the public via newspapers, television and the Internet with numerous appeals that helped to raise funds for aid. The same media gave far less attention to the earthquake that, the following year, devastated the remote Kashmir region of India and Pakistan, where few westerners were involved. As a result, much less money was collected for the victims of the earthquake.

The earthquake in Kashmir killed 87,000 people and displaced up to three million.

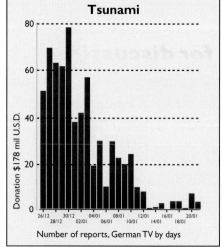

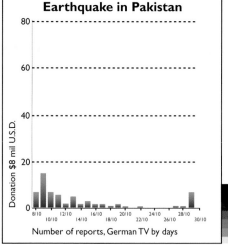

This graph shows how much money was donated in Germany to the victims of two disasters, and compares it to the number of TV reports on each.

12

Millions of people have died, and many more have lost their homes in the civil war in the Democratic Republic of Congo. Lack of media coverage can mean a lack of support for people in need.

The wrong people?

During other disasters, such as war and famine, the interest the media takes can again depend on more than how many people are involved and how much they are suffering. For example, the English-speaking media is usually more interested in Zimbabwe, which has a historical connection with Britain, than in the neighbouring, French-speaking Democratic Republic of Congo (DRC). The civil war in the DRC did get a brief period in the media spotlight in late 2008, but reports were soon overtaken by other news. Such media attention can greatly affect the amount of political support and aid a country and its people receive during times of crisis.

The UK government's minister for Africa, Lord Malloch-Brown, noticed that 'Political will goes ... up and down depending on the level of public and media concern.'

• Up for discussion •

Will people always be more interested in people and places that they know or can identify with? Why?

'Charity begins at home.' What do you think this means? Do you agree?

Raising the roof

Campaigners sometimes try to get maximum media attention for their cause by organising big public events such as demonstrations, meetings or concerts.

Case study: Live Aid and Live 8

The Live Aid campaign in 1985 was one of the biggest-ever media events of its kind. It was organised by the Irish musician and anti-poverty campaigner Bob Geldof to raise funds for famine relief in Ethiopia. There were two main concerts – one in New York and one in London – both of which were televised, and other smaller events around the world. Stars from the world of rock music took part, and over £110 million was raised.

For campaigning organisations, high-profile events like Live Aid help to make fundraising for their everyday work easier by raising public awareness. However, there is a risk that once the event is over, the media and the public may forget about the issues it raised.

The Live Aid concerts in 1985 brought the situation in Ethiopia, where millions were starving, to public notice, and raised millions of pounds.

Twenty years later, in 2005, Bob Geldof organised the 'Live 8' concerts. These took place simultaneously in each of the wealthy G8 nations, including the US, Britain, Japan and Germany. There was also a concert in South Africa. They were part of a campaign to put pressure on world leaders to 'make poverty history' by giving more international aid, cancelling countries' debts and finding a fairer way of organising world trade. Once again, celebrity musicians took part, performing to an audience of millions of people worldwide. Although the concerts could not, of course, succeed in ending world poverty, they did make the issues surrounding it better understood.

Global superstars like Madonna performed in the 2005 Live 8 concerts.

Follow-on

Other high-profile events include Nelson Mandela's 46664 campaign, which takes its name from his prison number when he was jailed for fighting for freedom in South Africa. This campaign aims to raise awareness about HIV/AIDS. Between 2003 and 2008, the campaign organised concerts in South Africa and other countries, with artists from all over the world taking part. Comedians have also banded together in several countries in local 'Comic Relief' campaigns to raise money for a range of causes.

• Up for discussion •

Do headline-grabbing events make it hard for less-known campaigns to compete?

What are the implications if a cause becomes fashionable for a while, but then stops getting media coverage?

The right face

Campaigners know that the media likes to report on a cause in terms of individual people. This can give the issue a personal touch, which helps people to remember it.

The right person

A charity for homeless people will tell one family's story, while an organisation raising funds for cancer research may show pictures of a patient who has recovered. The coverage is personal, but aims to make a general point, and so raise money for the many other people who need support.

Famous faces

Another way of linking a cause to a person is by seeking 'celebrity endorsement'. This is when a well-known person takes up a campaign and the media reports on it. The late Princess Diana was a famous example of this. The media loved her, and so gave massive coverage to her support of the campaign to ban the use of landmines. Her involvement played an important part in getting the cause noticed and in its eventual, partial, success.

Images such as these are used by charities to get the public to see people who struggle with problems such as poverty as individuals, and as real people.

Case study: Figureheads

All over the world, there are political regimes that deny whole groups of people the right to speak or act freely. Often, campaigners against these regimes will concentrate on the plight of an individual and use him or her as a case study for the media. The media uses such case studies to give a campaign a personal touch, so ordinary people can make a connection with it. The human rights organisation, Amnesty, has a long history of working this way – but other groups do the same.

For example, Aung San Suu Kyi, the democratically elected leader of Myanmar (Burma) is the world media's 'face' of her country's fight for democracy. She had been held under house arrest (not allowed to leave her home) by the military government for most of the time since 1989. In 2009, she was put on trial for breaching the terms of her house arrest. In many ways, Suu Kyi is identified with the struggle for freedom in her country.

• Up for discussion •

Is there a danger that the public will only be interested in a campaign if we like the person used as a 'face' for it? If so, why?

Aung San Suu Kyi has led the opposition to Myanmar's military government since her election in 1990.

A voice for
the voiceless

Campaigners throughout history have used the media to speak for people who cannot speak for themselves. These include the very poor, the sick, children and slaves.

Case study: Freedom for all

In the 1700s, anti-slavery campaigners used the media to build up sympathy for their cause. They published books and pamphlets, often with first-hand accounts from slaves themselves.

In the US, a runaway slave, Harriet Tubman, became famous for helping others escape from the plantations of the American south and for speaking out against slavery. Harriet Beecher Stowe's novel, Uncle Tom's Cabin (1852), also played a vital role in raising public awareness of slavery.

Harriet Tubman was born a slave in Maryland in the United States in around 1820. She wrote her autobiography, *Harriet Tubman, the Moses of Her People*, in 1869.

Helping children past...

As recently as the 19th century, it was commonly accepted that adults could treat children as they liked – for example, by making them work long, gruelling hours. Campaigners used the media to draw attention to and challenge this – such as when the famous author Charles Dickens described a child's life in a workhouse in *Oliver Twist* (1838), and in a factory in *David Copperfield* (1849–50).

An example of an early newspaper campaign for children was published in

1885. The London journalist W.T. Stead used the paper he edited, *The Pall Mall Gazette,* to highlight the issue of child prostitution with a series of articles in which he described how he had 'bought' a thirteen-year-old girl. The story was a media sensation and landed Stead in prison, but did eventually help to bring about better child protection laws.

... and present

In 2004, the International Labour Organization (ILO) estimated that around 218 million children were still working in factories in poorer parts of the world. Campaigners have used the media to draw public attention to companies that directly or indirectly use child labour – hoping to shame them into stopping. For example, in 2007, the British newspaper the *Observer* discovered that Indian child labour was involved in making clothes for suppliers to the US-based fashion chain, Gap. As a result, the Indian authorities were alerted and Gap took the clothes off the shelves.

• *Up for discussion* •

Occasionally, parts of the media attack campaigners against child labour. They say the issue is complicated and that poor families need the money their children earn. How would you answer this?

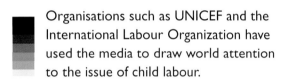

Organisations such as UNICEF and the International Labour Organization have used the media to draw world attention to the issue of child labour.

Two sides
to the story

Campaigners who oppose each other often carry out their arguments through the media, filling newspapers and television screens with dramatic imagery and language. This can be especially true when it comes to advances in science.

Science in the media

Explaining science in the media can be difficult for campaigners. Both sides use experts who can help the public to understand the facts and combat common myths and misunderstandings.

The stem cell debate

Medical researchers are looking into ways of using 'stem cells' taken from human embryos that have been created in a laboratory. These, they believe, could be used to help treat a whole range of conditions such as some forms of cancer and Parkinson's disease. Some evangelical Christian groups and the Catholic Church have opposed this technology, which they see as abortion, even murder. Parts of the media have supported this view – although experts in the field argue that stem cell technology is both acceptable and medically valuable.

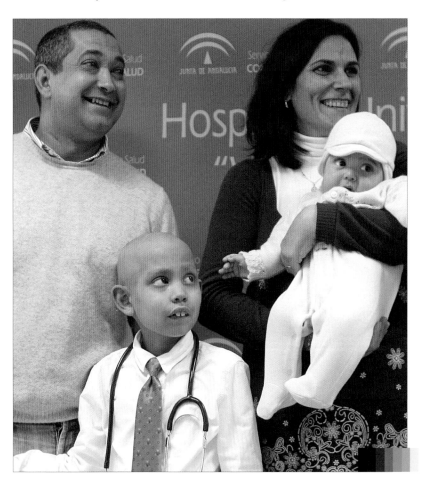

Stem calls taken from his baby brother Javier have helped to cure seven-year-old Andres (left) of a rare genetic disorder.

Case study: GM crops, for and against

An activist opposed to genetically modified (GM) crops tears up plants at a GM test crop site.

The subject of GM crops needs careful media explanation. These are crops that have been altered by science in a way that could not happen naturally, in order to raise yields or resist drought, pests or disease. The companies that make GM crops use PR to convince the public that the crops are useful and safe, and can be given additional nutritional benefits, as is the case with Golden Rice, a strain of rice that has been bred to include more vitamin A.

However, in much of Europe, many people are still suspicious. Opponents call the crops 'Frankenstein foods', after a 19th-century horror story in which a man created a monster. They argue in the media that GM crops can damage the environment by cross-breeding with wild plants. They also say that GM crops could damage the economies of poorer farming regions of the world. They accuse supporters of GM of over-emphasising the usefulness of the crops and overlooking the possible dangers.

• Up for discussion •

Choose a scientific issue and study the way the media covers campaigns around it. How can the media get the facts across clearly?

Conflicting causes

Often, the media has to report on conflicting sets of values, when the public is strongly divided about whether a cause is morally or politically right.

A question of values

Animal rights campaigners use the media to show pictures of suffering farm animals being reared intensively to attract public sympathy – but the producers argue that people want cheap meat. People living in beautiful countryside campaign in their local media against wind farms spoiling their landscape – while environmentalists believe this is a price we have to pay to end global warming.

Wind farms, such as this one in California in the US, provide clean, renewable energy, but many dislike their impact on the landscape.

A group of Muslim women and children demonstrate in Paris for the right to wear hijabs in state public schools.

Few issues are as hotly debated as that around the hijab (head covering) that many Muslim women wear. In France, the argument reached a peak in 2004 when the government banned 'religious symbols' from being worn in state schools. This covered Christian crosses and Jewish skullcaps, as well as hijabs. The government, and its supporters in the media, stressed that the ban reflected the French tradition of keeping religion out of education, and it was therefore not favouring any one faith over another.

Many people, including some Muslims, believed that the government was right. But because the media paid most attention to the hijab, some Muslims accused the government of running a campaign directed against Islam.

Anti-racist and human rights campaigners joined in. The US-based organisation Human Rights Watch said that the ban 'would violate the rights to freedom of religion and expression'. The French newspaper Le Monde *wrote that passing the law would lead to 'marginalising and excluding a part of the population' (Dec 2003).*

To anti-racist campaigners, all this looked like the media whipping up feeling specifically against Muslims.

• *Up for discussion* •

Would media coverage of the hijab debate be different in Muslim and non-Muslim countries? How might it differ?

Slow burn

Sometimes it takes years for the media to take an interest in a campaign. Fights to put right past injustices often fall into this category. Often, the first step is to convince the media – and the public – that a wrong has been done in the first place.

Out of sight...

In 1974, 21 people died in two bomb attacks in Birmingham. Afterwards, six men were found guilty of carrying out the bombing on behalf of the IRA (Irish Republican Army), which was fighting the British in Northern Ireland. The men were innocent – but it took a long time to convince the media and public of this. Campaigns in their support did not really take off for ten years, after TV programmes had been made about the case and the MP and author Chris Mullin published a book about it called *Error of Judgement* (1986). The men were finally freed in 1991.

The members of the Birmingham Six were finally freed in 1991, after 17 years of appeals and campaigning.

Case study: The Stolen Generations, Australia

Between about 1910 and 1970 in Australia, around 100,000 mixed-race Aboriginal children were taken from their parents and, mostly, raised in children's homes. Many white Australians saw this as 'rescuing' them from Aboriginal life.

Then, in 1981, a historian named Peter Read published a report called The Stolen Generations, showing the harm that had been done to the children and their families.

Read's opinion was supported by a national enquiry. In 2001, the story was brought to the world by a film – Rabbit Proof Fence – which told it through the eyes of two children. Most Australians now supported a formal apology to the Aboriginal people on behalf of the Australian government – but not all. As late as

2004, journalist Andrew Bolt still argued in Australia's Sunday Mail that there was no evidence of 'stolen' children – only abandoned ones. The apology came at last, in 2008, from Australian Prime Minister Kevin Rudd.

• Up for discussion •

Why do you think that the media take a long time to support some campaigns, or may never do so?

A scene from the 2001 film, Rabbit Proof Fence. The film helped to put pressure on the Australian government for an apology to the 'Stolen Generations'.

Straight talk

The media can play an important part in government campaigns to educate the public. These include, for example, encouraging healthy eating and taking exercise, or making people aware of the dangers and illegality, in most countries, of drinking alcohol and then driving.

Effective measures

Media campaigns against drink driving can be very effective. They may show, for example, pictures of people who were killed or badly injured by drunk drivers on TV or in newspapers and magazines. The June 2004 issue of the *American Journal of Preventive Medicine* suggested that these images can reduce alcohol-related car crashes by up to 13 per cent. Similar media campaigns have been used to encourage drivers to wear a seatbelt and to observe the speed limit.

Many countries have used the media to educate people about the dangers of drinking and driving, and so have saved many lives.

• Up for discussion •

What educational campaigns do you think are especially important for people in your age group?

HIV, the virus that causes AIDS, spreads mainly through sex. In sub-Saharan Africa, the disease took hold long before it was identified and an estimated 22 million people are infected. There is no cure, and treatment is very expensive, making education about prevention especially important. This can be hard because, in many countries, there is a tradition of not talking about sex. There are also misconceptions about how the illness is contracted.

The Ugandan government has risen to the challenge with a major media campaign using newspapers, billboards and radio. This has helped to bring infection rates down from an estimated 20 per cent to around 6 per cent. An organisation called Straight Talk has taken on the important job of communicating with young people. Straight Talk began in 1993 as a newspaper for 10–19-year-olds and now also offers information and counselling, produces informative radio programmes, publishes a magazine for primary schoolchildren and has an Internet presence.

In South Africa, where infection rates among adults are around 18 per cent, HIV has even been introduced into popular TV soap operas. Other countries, including Cambodia and India, also use soap operas to spread the word about HIV. In a survey in India, more than 70 per cent of people said that they had received their information about HIV and AIDS from television. Popular media coverage like this can save lives.

A campaigning sign in Zambia, Africa, reminds people that children become victims too when their parents die of AIDS.

The media
as campaigner

Sometimes, the media becomes a campaigner in its own right – but it may not always give the whole picture.

Getting it wrong?

'Megan's law' in the US is named after a child murdered in 1994 by a sex offender. It states that information about where known child abusers live must be made public. In Britain, the *News of the World* has campaigned for a similar law. But opponents believe that this encourages dangerous people to go into hiding, away from police supervision. They add that such laws overlook the fact that most abuse is carried out by people who the children already know.

The family of Megan Kanka watch the New Jersey governor sign a bill that will create an Internet register of sex offenders in the state.

In Britain, the early 2000s saw a huge media panic, involving newspapers, radio, television and the Internet. It was about the vaccination routinely given to children to prevent measles, mumps and rubella (MMR for short), and it followed an article in a medical journal that suggested the vaccination could trigger the condition autism. Almost no experts agreed – the Guardian's specialist science writer, Ben Goldacre, called it 'a hoax'. But parents were scared, vaccination levels dropped, and there was a dangerous rise in disease.

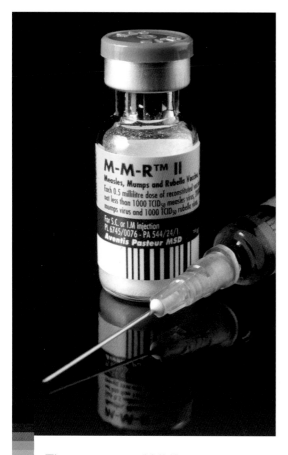

The controversial MMR vaccine.

Getting it right

Media campaigns can of course have positive results. In the 1950s and early 1960s, the drug thalidomide was given to pregnant women suffering from morning sickness. It was withdrawn in 1962, because it caused babies to be born with missing limbs and other health problems. In 1972, the *Sunday Times* campaigned to make thalidomide's British distributors pay high levels of compensation to affected families. The paper went on to show that thalidomide had not been tested properly, and claims were made against its manufacturer.

Campaigns elsewhere have had less success. German victims receive less than half the average amount of compensation paid in Britain. In Italy, Spain and Austria, victims have received nothing.

• Up for discussion •

What other media-led campaigns can you think of?

Which of these do you think were useful – and which less so? Why?

Making news

Campaigners can get media coverage for their cause by doing something dramatic to get noticed. This can include carrying out daring stunts, and even breaking the law.

Fighting fathers

Fathers 4 Justice is a group that campaigns for better access to children for divorced or separated fathers. It started in Britain, and now extends internationally. It is famous for stunts, which have included climbing the London Eye and scaling Buckingham Palace. Critics say the stunts do the cause more harm than good. But there is no doubt they get media attention.

Green campaigners

The environmental campaigning organisation Greenpeace has a history of making dramatic gestures. In recent years, it has drawn attention to the damaging effects of greenhouse gases, which almost all scientists believe are causing the Earth's climate to change and get warmer (see page 38-39). Greenpeace members have blockaded coal-burning power stations and, in 2008, dumped coal outside a hotel in Warsaw, the capital of Poland, during an important international meeting about the future of coal. They also floated a huge balloon over a coal-fired power station in Australia, with the slogan 'No future in coal'.

Three members of Fathers 4 Justice, dressed as superheroes Captain America, Batman and Robin, protest on a ledge outside the UK Foreign Office.

Greenpeace members at work building a replica of Noah's Ark on the slopes of Mount Ararat, where tradition says the Ark ended its journey, to draw attention to climate change.

• *Up for discussion* •

Why is a stunt, which may break the law and even be dangerous, a good way to get media attention?

Can stunts result in bad media coverage? Can this harm a cause or campaign?

Case study: 'An Inconvenient Truth'

In 2006, former US Vice-President Al Gore was so concerned by US attitudes to climate change that he made his own dramatic gesture by making a film about it: 'An Inconvenient Truth'. At the time, the US government was sympathetic to the tiny minority of scientists that doubts that climate change really is the result of human activity. The US media gave air-time and space to these doubters, claiming that they were being balanced and leading the public to believe that the causes of climate change really are open to question. Gore's film, along with a website and meetings addressed by Gore himself, aimed to challenge the doubters – and to get people to act.

Scare tactics

'It [Chernobyl] was the worst nuclear accident … ever seen …
The fallout, 400 times more radioactivity than … at Hiroshima, drove a
third of a million people from their homes and triggered an epidemic of
thyroid cancer ….' (*National Geographic, April 2006*).

Case study: Nuclear fear

*The explosion at the Chernobyl nuclear plant,
Ukraine, in April 1986 was the industry's worst
nightmare. But campaigners had long warned
of the dangers of nuclear power. A film called
'The China Syndrome' (1979) dramatised
the possibility of an accident only months
before a real-life near-disaster at Three Mile
Island nuclear plant in Pennsylvania, USA.*

*No one knows how many deaths Chernobyl has
caused over the years from the effects of
radiation. One Greenpeace estimate was
90,000. Other estimates ran into millions.*

*Public fears make it easy for anti-nuclear
campaigners to get coverage for other
concerns, such as the problem of radiation
leaks, and the difficulty of storing highly
dangerous nuclear waste
safely. In many countries, such
campaigns have had a certain
amount of success. In Sweden,
for example, safety issues have
led the authorities to decide –
at least for now – to phase out
nuclear power.*

A reactor at Chernobyl nuclear
power station exploded on
April 26, 1986, releasing
dangerous radioactive material
into the atmosphere.

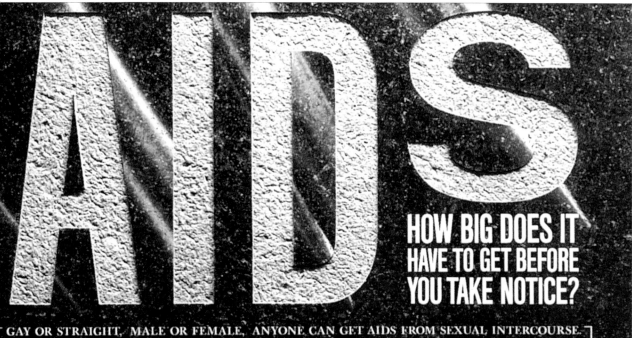

AIDS

HOW BIG DOES IT HAVE TO GET BEFORE YOU TAKE NOTICE?

GAY OR STRAIGHT, MALE OR FEMALE, ANYONE CAN GET AIDS FROM SEXUAL INTERCOURSE. SO THE MORE PARTNERS, THE GREATER THE RISK. PROTECT YOURSELF. USE A CONDOM.

'Crying wolf'?

In the early 1980s, the world first learned about AIDS. Governments in many countries responded with huge campaigns, warning the population of an epidemic that could, in the words of a British television advertisement, 'kill through ignorance'. Scare stories about AIDS still circulate – with lurid tales of people 'deliberately' infecting others.

But how effective are scare stories? The massive AIDS epidemic in western Europe and the US has still not happened – although it certainly has in Africa. Similarly, supporters of nuclear power say that its dangers have been exaggerated. If messages seem to be overplayed, is there a danger that people will start to ignore them – or doubt them altogether?

This 1986 television advert aimed to get people to change their behaviour as a response to AIDS. Some critics think that the adverts did more harm than good, as people stopped reacting to scare tactics.

• Up for discussion •

How can we judge whether things are as bad as the media – or a campaign, using the media – says they are?

Giving the people what they want?

Media outlets tend to have an idea about who their audience is and what they will be interested in. This can affect the way they report – or do not report – on a whole range of issues.

Case study: War and anti-war

There has been much criticism of the war in Iraq. But anti-war campaigners complain that it can be difficult to get their views heard in the media.

The war against Afghanistan began in 2001, after terrorists attacked New York and Washington DC on 11 September. The US government believed that Osama Bin Laden, the leader of al Qaeda, the group that made the attacks, was being sheltered in Afghanistan.

Two years later, the US and some other countries, including Britain, attacked Iraq because, they said, it had weapons of mass destruction. This was later found to be untrue. In the US, some government officials even (wrongly) claimed that there were links between the government of Iraq and Al Qaeda – a view reported by, among others, the television network Fox News.

Demonstrations against the war in Iraq took place all over the world and were widely reported in the media. However, once the war was underway, the anti-war movement claimed that it became harder to get media attention. One explanation for this may be that many media outlets believe the public wants to support soldiers in Iraq in their mission. They therefore may choose not to include stories or reports that appear to criticise it.

Fear of terrorism

Fear of terrorism since the 9/11 attacks has encouraged governments to pass laws restricting people's freedoms. In the US and Britain, suspected terrorists have been deported, or imprisoned for periods of time without proper trials. Campaigners for human rights find it difficult to get the media to support challenges to this. The media goes along with – even supports – what it feels is public opinion.

• *Up for discussion* •

Should the media take any notice of public or government opinion? Why?

Is it possible for the media to cover a controversial campaign and not take sides about it? How?

In the aftermath of 9/11, many al Qaeda suspects were held by the US military at Guantanamo Bay naval base in Cuba.

A bad light

Sometimes, the media seems to run or join in with campaigns of hostility towards certain groups of people – and anyone who dares to speak up for them.

Immigration

Immigrants, especially those who arrive as refugees, are often faced with media hostility. Australia's Refugee Council, for example, reports that 'Refugees, asylum seekers and the Australians who support them have had to endure countless media articles full of inaccuracies … sometimes media organisations … publish information which is blatantly false.'

In Britain, some newspapers behave in a similar way, with articles headed 'Asylum seekers use your taxes to smuggle in relatives' and 'Asylum seekers get free holidays' (both from the *Daily Express*). Such coverage can make it hard for the public to get a fair picture – though, as always when groups of people are persecuted or treated badly, supportive pressure groups do exist.

Immigrant Mexican workers in California. Immigrants often suffer prejudice from local people who are afraid that the newcomers will take their jobs. The media often encourages this attitude.

Case study: The Roma people

A Roma settlement in Italy. The Roma often suffer discrimination in housing, employment and education, and many live in poverty.

In the 700 years since the ethnic group known as the Roma (once called 'gypsies') arrived in Europe from India, they have been romanticised in songs and stories. But they have also been accused of being thieves, pickpockets, kidnappers – even murderers. During World War II, around 600,000 Roma were killed in concentration camps. It is a reflection of the media attitude to the Roma that this tragedy is often forgotten today.

Media coverage of Roma issues continues this tradition. For example, in Italy in 2007, the media did little to challenge politicians who suggested that the Roma – including Italian Roma – should be deported, even after Roma homes were attacked.

Elsewhere in Europe, where the Roma usually live in the poorest housing with high levels of unemployment, little effort is made by the media to challenge the racism the Roma suffer. In fact, the media often makes it worse –

as, for example, in 1991, in the Polish town of Mawa, when a local radio station accused a young Roma man of running away after a fatal car accident. Local papers repeated this and a group of townspeople attacked the local Roma community for five days.

• Up for discussion •

What examples can you find of popular campaigns against groups of people? What part does the media play in these campaigns?

Taking on the media

How can campaigners take on the media, when it seems to be working against them? How can they get media coverage when the big media outlets are just not interested?

Hard to be heard

We have seen how newspapers, television and radio often report in ways that can seem unfair. This may be because a pressure group has paid large sums of money to get its view across, or simply because the media is unwilling to concentrate on anything – including campaigns and causes – that it thinks few people care about. Instead, it may support campaigns that seem unfair or wrong.

Uphill work

Challenging the way the media behaves can be hard, and campaigners may struggle to get their voices heard if their cause is considered unpopular or not interesting. When such campaigns do get a hearing, it may not be in the top-selling newspapers or national television programmes. It will usually be in papers and magazines and programmes that reach only people with a special interest in the campaign, or others like it.

However, even unpopular causes can get heard – eventually. Gradually, the popular media may start to listen. This has happened, for example, with campaigns centred around the environment. Once,

Powerful images such as this, showing polar bears stranded on melting pack ice, have helped campaigners convince the media to support their views on climate change.

Case study: Regulating the media

There are organisations in many countries that keep a watchful eye on media reporting. One is the US organisation FAIR, which describes itself as 'a national media watch group, … scrutinizing media practices that marginalize public interest, minority and dissenting viewpoints'. It runs a magazine called EXTRA! and its own radio show. In Britain, there is the Campaign for Press and Broadcasting Freedom:

'an independent voice for media reform … (working) … to promote policies for diverse and democratic media.' Also in Britain, a group called Mediawise campaigns on behalf of people who have suffered as a result of media coverage. It also provides guidance for journalists covering sensitive subjects – as does the US-based DART Center for Journalism and Trauma.

Campaigning organisations within the media work towards making sure that coverage of events such as war is fair and accurate, and as sensitive as possible.

these were given little media coverage, and were even treated as a joke. Now, they are widely accepted because the facts surrounding climate change are becoming more widely known and understood.

• Up for discussion •

How can campaigners get their views across to parts of the media that don't agree with them?

Can you think of any campaigns that have challenged or even changed the way the media covers certain issues?

Make the media
work for you

Campaigning can be hard work and takes time. But it is now possible for people – even those with few resources – to launch their own campaigns.

Internet campaigning

Using the Internet, with user-generated video sites, such as YouTube, it is possible for campaigners to produce their films and share them with thousands of people. Social networking sites such as Facebook and Twitter can also be used. So can simply emailing supporters to tell them about what a campaign is doing and guiding them to websites and blogs that carry news, or keeping in touch using text messages.

The Avaaz organisation, for example, updates millions of supporters all over the world by email alert, giving news about its campaign 'to close the gap between the world we have, and the world most people everywhere want'. The US-based group 'Move on.org' came to prominence during the Internet anti-war campaign and has branched out into a range of campaigns on other issues, including reform of the media. The Internet can be a powerful tool for campaigning. However, it is often best to use a combination of different media, both to draw attention to issues and to follow them up.

Handwritten messages to President Obama fill a wall erected by the Avaaz group in Washington DC.

An example of a campaign that has been widely reported in the news media, but which also makes good use of the Internet, is the search for Madeleine McCann.

Four-year-old Madeleine vanished from a holiday apartment in Portugal in May 2007. The story of her parents' search for her remained in the news for months.

The media coverage was not always sympathetic, and was sometimes inaccurate. But it did mean that it was almost impossible for anyone not to know about Madeleine. Since the disappearance, Madeleine's parents have used the Internet to raise funds to help in the search for their missing daughter, and to publish news about it, as well as pictures of Madeleine. They have worked to keep the story in the news in the hope that they will one day learn the truth about what happened to their little girl.

When four-year-old Madeleine McCann was abducted from a holiday apartment in Portugal, her parents launched a worldwide media campaign to find her.

• *Up for discussion* •

Find out about campaigns run by young people and how they have used the media and created their own media coverage using the Internet.

Glossary

Aboriginal The earliest inhabitants of a region – in this case, the people who lived in Australia before the first settlers from Europe arrived.

AIDS Acquired Immune Deficiency Syndrome. It is a disease that destroys a person's ability to fight infections.

Animal rights Opposition to using animals for research, keeping them cruelly, and so on.

Campaign Organised activities aimed at getting a change in the way governments or people in general behave.

Cause A movement that people support and campaign for.

Civil war War between two or more groups of people in a single country.

Climate change A shift in the world's climate.

Compensation A payment or other award given to someone has suffered a loss or injury.

Demonstration A march or big meeting held to draw attention to an issue.

Deport To expel someone from a country.

Embryo A human in its early stages of development, before it is born.

Epidemic A widespread infectious disease.

Global warming The gradual warming of the Earth's climate.

GM crops Crops that have been altered by scientists so that they contain genes that would not occur in the crop naturally.

Hijab A special kind of head covering worn by some Muslim women.

Human rights Our rights as human beings: the United Nations has published a Universal Declaration of Human Rights which lists them.

Immigrant A person who comes into a foreign country or region to live.

International aid Funds given by one country to another for help in times of difficulty.

Media The methods we use to communicate – including newspapers, radio, television, film, magazines, books and the Internet.

Nuclear reactor The part of a nuclear power station where atoms are 'split' to make the energy used in the power station.

Persecute To treat a person or group of people, often because of their race or religion.

Public relations The job of communicating the work of an organisation to the media.

Press release A written communication to the media, informing them about an event that has happened or is about to happen.

Pressure group A group that tries to influence public opinion and policy-making, in particular government policy-making.

Radioactivity The energy created when atoms are broken or 'split'.

Radiation Energy in the form of particles or electromagnetic waves. In larger doses, radiation can be harmful to humans.

Refugee Someone who flees from their home or country, often because of war.

Roma The proper name for the people once called Gypsies. They are descended from a group of people who left India between the 1000s and 1400s and settled in much of Europe. Traditionally, they were nomads, but many are now settled.

Rubella A disease caused by a virus. It is often called German Measles. If a pregnant woman catches it, it can harm her unborn child.

Stem cell A body cell that can develop into any other kind of body cell.

Terrorism Carrying out violent attacks for political reasons.

Tsunami A huge wave in the ocean that forms after an earthquake.

Vaccination Infecting someone with a very mild form of a germ that causes disease, so that their body is able to fight off the germs in future. It is also called immunisation.

Wind farm A group of wind turbines (motors with large blades that turn in the wind). They are used to generate electricity using energy from the wind.

Further information

Books

Campaigns for Change series by Sean Connolly (Franklin Watts, 2007)

Great Britons: Campaigners for Change by Ann Kramer (Franklin Watts, 2007)

Behind the News: Human Rights: Who Decides? by Ann Kramer (Heinemann Education, 2007)

What's Your View? The Power of the Media by Adam Hibbert (Franklin Watts, 2006)

Websites

www.unicef.org/righttoknow/index_mediacampaign. html
Advice from the UN children's organisation on how to start a media campaign.

www.ilo.org/ipec/lang–en/index.htm
The International Labour Organization campaign against child labour.

www.guardian.co.uk/world/2004/feb/04/schools. schoolsworldwide
About the issue of the Muslim veil in France

www.romani.org
A website about the Roma people.

www.broadcasthivafrica.org
A website promoting information about and protection from HIV/AIDS across Africa.

www.timesonline.co.uk/tol/life_and_style/health/article 4818160.ece
The story of the Thalidomide campaign.

www.climatecrisis.net
About Al Gore's film, 'An Inconvenient Truth'.

www.humanrights.gov.au/social_justice/bth_report/ about/who_spoke_out.html
Tells the story of the Stolen Generations.

www.cpbf.org.uk
www.fair.org/index.php
The UK and US campaigns for a better media.

www.mediawise.org.uk
Advice, information, research and training on media ethics.

http://pol.moveon.org
'MoveOn is a service – a way for … citizens to find their political voice in a system dominated by big money and big media.'

Note to parents and teachers: Every effort has been made by the Publishers to ensure that these websites are suitable for children, that they are of the highest educational value, and that they contain no inappropriate or offensive material. However, because of the nature of the Internet, it is impossible to guarantee that the contents of these sites will not be altered. We strongly advise that Internet access is supervised by a responsible adult.

Index

These are the list of contents for each title in *Media Power*.